# INTEGRITY RISKS AND RED FLAGS IN
# TRANSPORT PROJECTS

JANUARY 2023

**ADB**

ASIAN DEVELOPMENT BANK

Notes:
References in this publication to bidders, bids, bid evaluation committees, and bid evaluation
reports are used within the context of the procurement of works (contractors), goods (suppliers),
and consulting and non-consulting services.

All photos by ADB except when otherwise stated.

In this publication, "$" refers to United States dollars.

On the cover: **Transport in the Philippines**. An electric tricycle quietly rides along Legazpi Bay,
Albay (photo by Al Benavente).

Cover design by Paolo Tan.

# CONTENTS

# TABLES, FIGURE, BOXES, AND CHECKLISTS

## TABLES

## FIGURE

## BOXES

## CHECKLISTS

# FOREWORD

Since 2003, the Asian Development Bank's Office of Anticorruption and Integrity has conducted proactive integrity reviews (PIRs) to identify and address control weaknesses that give rise to integrity risks in ongoing sovereign operations. Insights from these PIRs are published in this series, *Integrity Risks and Red Flags*.

This publication highlights weaknesses and red flags identified through PIRs of 31 transport projects financed by ADB. Further volumes in the series feature insights from five other sectors: agriculture, natural resources, and rural development; education; energy; health; and water. Through this sector-based series, governments, public bodies, and stakeholders engaged in designing and implementing projects can learn from past vulnerabilities and establish processes and controls to effectively mitigate integrity risks.

To help foster and sustain economic growth, ADB's Strategy 2030 underscores the strengthening of governance and institutional capacity as an operational priority in the bank's developing member countries. Let us achieve a prosperous, inclusive, resilient, and sustainable Asia and the Pacific by maintaining the highest ethical standards.

**John Versantvoort**
Head, Office of Anticorruption and Integrity
Asian Development Bank

# ACKNOWLEDGMENTS

*Integrity Risks and Red Flags in Transport Projects* was prepared and developed collaboratively by H. Lorraine Wang (former advisor), Caridad Garrido Ortega (consultant and former senior integrity specialist), and Erickson Quijano (consultant) of the Preventive and Compliance Division, Office of Anticorruption and Integrity, Asian Development Bank.

This publication greatly benefited from the insights and comments of John Versantvoort (head), David Binns (former advisor), Lisa Kelaart-Courtney (director), Jung Min Han (senior integrity specialist), and Kristopher Marasigan (integrity officer) of the Office of Anticorruption and Integrity. This publication was made possible by the reviews from David Robinett (senior public management specialist – State Owned Enterprise Reforms, Sustainable Development and Climate Change Department [SDCC]); Michael Anyala (senior road management specialist, SDCC); Robert Valkovic (former principal transport specialist, SDCC); Jamie Leather (chief, Transport Sector Group, SDCC); Renadi Budiman (principal portfolio management specialist, Southeast Asia Department); Julian Doczi (procurement specialist, Procurement, Portfolio, and Financial Management Department [PPFD]); Aman Trana (chief financial management officer, PPFD); Eisuke Tajima (principal education specialist, Central and West Asia Department); and Maria Theresa Villareal (unit head - Portfolio Management, Pacific Department).

# ABBREVIATIONS

| | |
|---|---|
| ADB | Asian Development Bank |
| BEC | bid evaluation committee |
| BER | bid evaluation report |
| DMC | developing member country |
| OAI | Office of Anticorruption and Integrity |
| PIR | proactive integrity review |

# INTRODUCTION

Since the Asian Development Bank (ADB) adopted its Anticorruption Policy in 1998, fighting corruption has become embedded in ADB's broader work in governance, public administration, and capacity development.[1] The Anticorruption Policy affirms the bank's zero tolerance for corruption and lays the groundwork for supporting anticorruption efforts.

ADB's Strategy 2030 identifies strengthening governance and institutional capacity as one of seven operational priorities for a prosperous, inclusive, resilient, and sustainable Asia and the Pacific. The Office of Anticorruption and Integrity (OAI) promotes the implementation of this operational priority through a combination of activities aimed at (i) enforcement and (ii) prevention and compliance.

The proactive integrity review (PIR) is a mechanism used by ADB since 2003 to help prevent and detect integrity violations and address risks in ADB-financed or -administered projects. PIRs (i) identify and assess integrity risks in procurement, contract and asset management, and financial management of a project; and (ii) recommend measures to mitigate these risks to ensure that project funds are used for their intended purposes.

PIRs evaluate the adherence of projects to three core principles of project integrity: (i) transparency—proper documentation of key decisions, public disclosure of project information, and protection of confidential information; (ii) fairness—objective and reliable bidding process and requirements optimizing competition, impartial evaluation, and a credible complaints mechanism; and (iii) accountability and control—accurate and timely project accounting and reporting, eligibility of expenditures and timely payments, adherence to contract provisions, and adequate project oversight and management.

OAI ensures that PIR knowledge is applied to the projects reviewed through follow-up reviews, at which time OAI verifies the implementation status of the PIR. In addition, OAI assists the executing and implementing agencies in addressing open recommendations.[2]

PIR knowledge is institutionalized in ADB operations through (i) embedding of PIR requirements in ADB guidance and instruction documents, (ii) integrity risk management reviews, (iii) knowledge enhancement and transfer workshops and other learning courses, and (iv) knowledge products.[3] Following a country-focused approach (one of three guiding principles outlined in Strategy 2030), PIR knowledge also informs the country partnership strategies of developing member countries (DMCs).[4] Through this exercise, PIR knowledge is considered in designing new projects as the country partnership strategy predominantly drives country operations business plans.

This publication presents vulnerabilities from PIRs of 31 transport projects (Appendix) across 17 countries and 5 regions, and highlights recommended measures to mitigate identified integrity risks.[5]

---

[1] ADB. 1998. *Anticorruption Policy*. Manila.

[2] The follow-up review reports document the implementation status of PIR recommendations (footnote 5).

[3] Through integrity risk management reviews, PIR knowledge is built in preapproval project documents (concept papers, reports and recommendations of the President to the Board of Directors, technical assistance reports).

[4] The country partnership strategy is the primary platform for defining ADB's operational focus in a developing member country.

[5] The transport projects reviewed were selected from all active ADB-financed loan and grant projects using a risk-based selection process. The selection process took into account the size of funding, lending modality, implementation arrangements, number of awarded contracts, level of disbursements, input from relevant ADB departments, prior project results, external benchmarking, and potential benefits of a PIR to the project. PIR reports are available on the ADB website (*https://www.adb.org/who-we-are/integrity/proactive-integrity-review*).

# SECTOR OVERVIEW

Transport is an integral support, conveying goods and services to improve people's lives. ADB assists its DMCs in building infrastructure and services that contribute toward low-carbon emissions and safe, accessible, and affordable transport systems.

Transport has been one of ADB's main sectors over the last 4 decades with transport operations accounting

for nearly 32% of total ADB lending. Since 1966, ADB has financed $35.6 billion in transport investments.

Table 1 presents ADB's financial resources commitments in the transport sector from 2017 to 2021.

### Table 1: ADB's Financing Commitments in the Transport Sector, 2017–2021

| YEAR | 2017 | 2018 | 2019 | 2020 | 2021 |
|---|---|---|---|---|---|
| Value ($ million) | 5,058 | 4,957 | 7,536 | 3,147 | 3,396 |
| Percent of commitments in all sectors | 23.21% | 20.22% | 31.38% | 9.96% | 14.92% |

ADB = Asian Development Bank.
Source: ADB. 2022. ADB Annual Report 2021. Manila.

# INTEGRITY RISKS AND RED FLAGS

## Methodology

OAI identified and synthesized integrity-related vulnerabilities, including red flags, from all its transport PIR findings.[6] A vulnerability is any gap in a project's implementation processes that, if not remedied in a timely manner, will increase the likelihood of an integrity violation occurring and/or the impact of an integrity violation. In other words, the vulnerability increases the risk profile of the project.

Integrity risk is the risk that project funds are diverted from their intended purposes due to fraud, corruption, and other integrity violations.[7] Integrity violations are more likely to occur if integrity risks are not identified and addressed effectively and in a timely manner. Integrity risk management is an essential prerequisite for ensuring that projects achieve the intended development outcomes.

OAI assessed the level of vulnerabilities (high, medium, or low) by occurrence and impact.[8] This publication follows the project implementation processes and related subprocesses shown in Table 2. It also describes high- and medium-risk vulnerabilities and mitigating measures in each project implementation process.

## Table 2: Project Implementation Processes

| Process | | |
|---|---|---|
| **Procurement** | **Contract and Asset Management** | **Financial Management** |
| **A1 Bidding** <br> Prequalification, bidding documents preparation, bid advertisements, submissions, and opening | **B1 Contract administration** <br> The management of the day-to-day practicalities and administrative requirements under the contract | **C1 Expenditure management** <br> Approval and processing of payments for project expenditures |
| **A2 Bid evaluation** <br> Assessment of bidders' compliance with bidding requirements, and preparation and approval of evaluation report | **B2 Output monitoring** <br> Engagement with/supervision of contractors, consultants, and suppliers in relation to project outputs | **C2 Financial reporting** <br> Project accounting and auditing |
| **A3 Contract award** <br> Post-bid evaluation activities until contract is awarded and signed | **B3 Asset control** <br> Safeguarding and maintenance of project assets including asset inventory | |

Note: The subprocesses reflect those prioritized by the Office of Anticorruption and Integrity and do not reflect all subprocesses that exist within each process.

Source: Office of Anticorruption and Integrity, Asian Development Bank.

---

[6] Red flags are indicators of irregularities, which may indicate the occurrence of integrity violations. Project staff should be alert to red flags of integrity violations for them to promptly report potential violations to OAI.

[7] Integrity violation is any act which violates ADB's Anticorruption Policy, including corrupt, fraudulent, coercive, or collusive practice; abuse; conflict of interest; and obstructive practice. Other integrity violations include violations of ADB sanctions, retaliation against whistleblowers and witnesses, and other violations of ADB's Anticorruption Policy, including failure to adhere to the highest ethical standards.

[8] OAI determined the occurrence of a vulnerability by establishing the frequency with which this was identified in the PIRs; and based the impact of a vulnerability on the likelihood that this could have resulted in an integrity violation or misuse of project funds.

# Integrity Risk Heat Maps

The heat map in Figure (a) shows the level of risk arising from vulnerabilities identified in the transport PIRs and presented in the processes in which they manifested.[9] In the 31 transport projects reviewed, OAI identified high integrity risks in the procurement and financial management processes.

Figure (b) shows the risk level by subprocess. Risk levels are highest in bidding (A1) and bid evaluation (A2) subprocesses.

## Figure: Integrity Risk Heat Maps

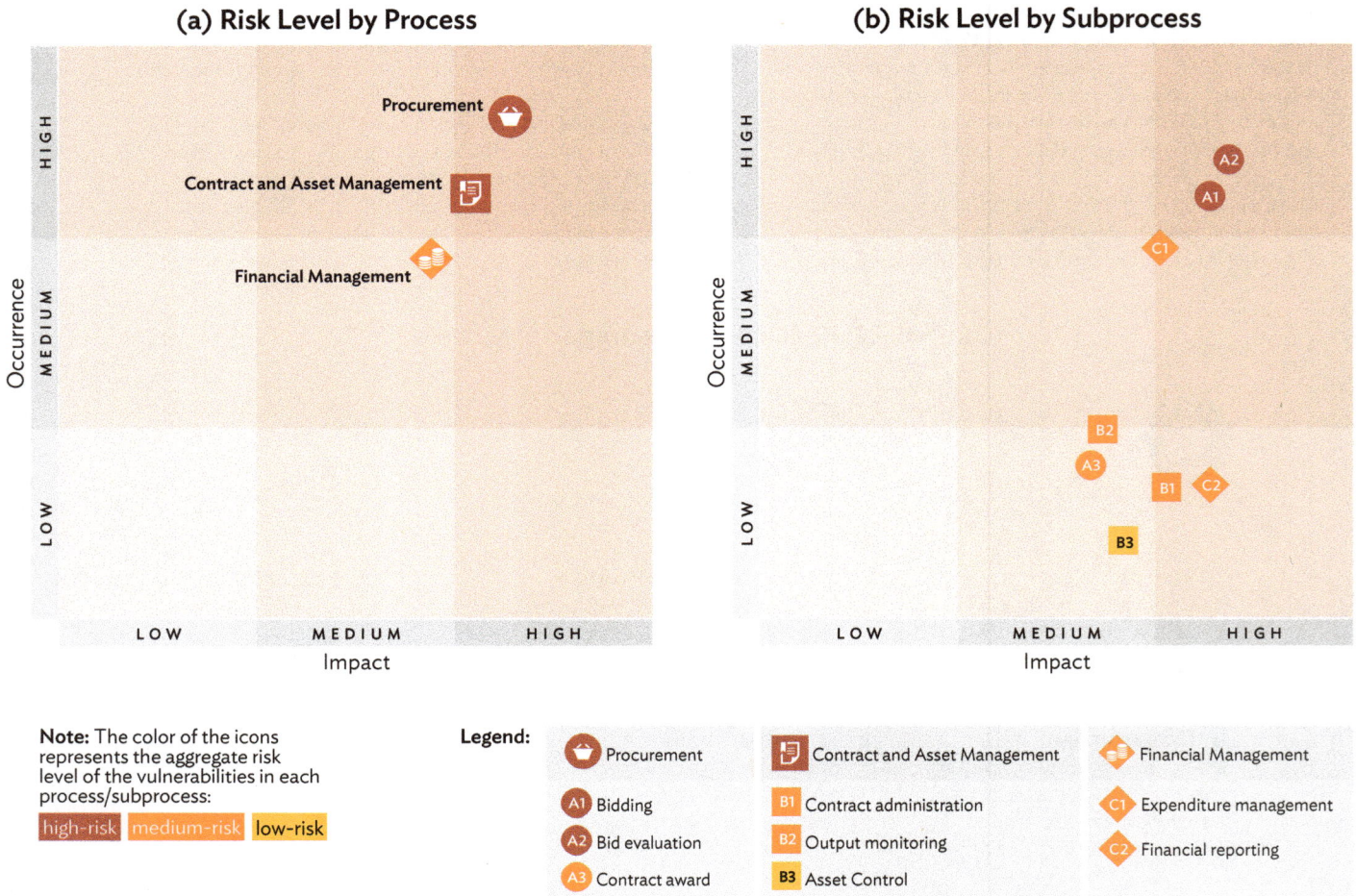

### (a) Risk Level by Process

### (b) Risk Level by Subprocess

**Note:** The color of the icons represents the aggregate risk level of the vulnerabilities in each process/subprocess:

high-risk    medium-risk    low-risk

**Legend:**

| | | |
|---|---|---|
| Procurement | Contract and Asset Management | Financial Management |
| A1 Bidding | B1 Contract administration | C1 Expenditure management |
| A2 Bid evaluation | B2 Output monitoring | C2 Financial reporting |
| A3 Contract award | B3 Asset Control | |

Source: Office of Anticorruption and Integrity, Asian Development Bank.

---

9    The heat map is a visual representation of relationships among two sets of data: the likelihood that an integrity violation may occur (occurrence) and its potential impact to the project (impact).

# Vulnerabilities and Mitigating Measures

OAI's analysis aimed to identify factors contributing to integrity vulnerabilities and to formulate risk mitigating measures. These measures may be applied to all projects regardless of their financing modality or structure. Project teams can use the due diligence checklists during bid evaluation (Checklist 1) and expenditure payment processing (Checklist 2) to identify and mitigate integrity risks.[10]

## PROCUREMENT

### (A1) Bidding

*Red flags of integrity violations.* OAI identified red flags indicating that the fairness of the bidding process may have been undermined. These increase the likelihood of occurrence of fraud and corruption that may jeopardize the project and alienate prospective bidders. Examples of red flags in bidding are summarized in Table 3.

Red flags are multifaceted, and may have one or a combination of the elements of collusion, fraud, corruption, and/or conflicts of interest.

### Table 3: Examples of Red Flags in Bidding

| Type of Integrity Violation | Red Flags |
|---|---|
| Collusive practice | **Similarities in bids**<br>• Bidders submitted the same unit prices for the same items in the bills of quantities.<br>• Bidders submitted sequential bid securities issued by the same bank. |
| | **Losing bidders have nonexistent contact numbers**<br>Losing bidders did not provide contact numbers or provided nonworking contact numbers. |
| | **Limited number of bids in each lot**<br>For a civil works package consisting of 10 lots, there was only one bidder who submitted a bid for each lot, and the bidder then became the winner. |
| Conflict of interest | **Contracting party failed to disclose conflict of interest**<br>A former ADB staff who had been primarily involved in the processing of a project was engaged as a consultant for the same project after retiring from ADB. |
| | **Close associations with a vendor**<br>One of the key officers of the consulting firm was said to be related to, or have close relationships with government officials and related ministers that were involved in awarding of the contract. |

ADB = Asian Development Bank.

Notes: 1. Collusive practice is an arrangement between two or more parties designed to achieve an improper purpose, including influencing improperly the actions of another party.

2. Conflict of interest is any situation in which a party has interests that could improperly influence a party's performance of official duties or responsibilities, contractual obligations, or compliance with applicable laws and regulations.

Source: Office of Anticorruption and Integrity, Asian Development Bank.

---

[10] OAI rolled out project management checklists to help executing and implementing agencies to self-assess (i) executing/implementing agency capacity, (ii) project procurement processes, (iii) financial management, and (iv) project output management from an integrity perspective. These checklists are available at https://www.adb.org/who-we-are/integrity/proactive-integrity-review.

PROCUREMENT

CONTRACT
AND ASSET
MANAGEMENT

FINANCIAL
MANAGEMENT

OTHER
VULNERABILITIES

**MITIGATING MEASURES**
Red Flags of Integrity Violations

- ADB regional departments and resident missions should ensure that executing and/or implementing agencies, including project implementing units and/or offices and evaluation committees, understand their obligations under ADB's Anticorruption Policy, especially the obligation to report any integrity violation to OAI when such allegation is initially identified or suspected. Executing and/or implementing agencies should communicate these obligations to the bidders (contractors, consultants, suppliers); provide the necessary oversight; and conduct appropriate due diligence to minimize the risk of integrity violations on development projects.

- The executing agency should (i) establish procedures for all executing and implementing agency staff to disclose real or perceived conflict of interest with any bidders or other parties involved in the project and (ii) actively monitor its staff integrity and require them to adhere to the highest ethical standards.

## (A2) Bid Evaluation

Vulnerabilities in bid evaluation can result in contracts awarded to unqualified bidders, thereby undermining the transparency and fairness of the procurement at an ultimate cost to the project. Process inconsistencies and deficiencies, and inaccurate evaluation results may create the impression of favoring bidders. If not addressed, these vulnerabilities may eventually lead to substandard outputs, delayed implementation, waste, loss of funds, or harm to the intended beneficiaries.

*Inadequate due diligence.* Bidders may provide dubious information on their eligibility, financial capacity, and experience. Without adequate due diligence during bid evaluation, bid evaluation committees (BECs) may fail to identify irregularities, inconsistencies, and/or potential misrepresentation.

Following a risk-based approach, the BEC should conduct due diligence to verify the submitted bid information against supporting documents (records check), from online sources (sanctions and other desktop research including previous adverse news), and/or from third parties (reference check). Combined with professional attributes such as a questioning mind and a critical assessment of documents, due diligence requires looking for indications of errors/misrepresentations on the documents, including checking the accuracy of information drawn from computations. The BEC should also seek clarifications/substantiation from bidders to the extent allowed by the bidding documents.

Examples of these evaluation errors resulting from the lack of or inadequate due diligence are summarized in Table 4. Box 1 presents sample cases of bid evaluation errors.

## Table 4: Examples of Evaluation Errors

| Bid Evaluation Aspect/Requirement | Nature of Evaluation Error |
|---|---|
| Financial capacity | **Average annual construction turnover**<br>• The bid evaluation committee (BEC) used the bidders' turnover figures indicated in their bid forms, which were higher than the figures in the submitted audited financial statements. ⚠<br>• The BEC did not seek clarification from a bidder whose bidding form indicated a turnover figure that was higher than in the prequalification forms for the same year.<br><br>**Working capital and net worth**<br>• The BEC used the bidder's net worth and working capital declared in the bidding forms, which were greater than the corresponding amounts in the submitted audited financial statements. ⚠<br>• The BEC did not consider current liabilities in the evaluation of bidders' available financial resources, resulting in overstatement of the bidders' working capital.<br>• The BEC did not seek clarifications from the bidder on the declaration of total assets, which did not tally with the bidder's combined liabilities and net worth.<br>• The BEC accepted the bidders' expired credit lines or credit lines that were conditional upon a trigger event.<br>• The BEC considered the figures of the consolidated financial statements when the stand-alone audited financial statements of the bidder should have been used.<br><br>**Current contract commitments**<br>• The BEC did not seek clarifications from the bidder whose current contract commitments declared in prequalification submissions were not declared in the bids (post-qualification). ⚠<br>• The BEC used the bidder's current contract commitment amounts declared in the bids, which were lower than the figures indicated in the supporting documents. The BEC did not seek clarifications from the bidder on the discrepancies noted. ⚠ |
| Experience | • The BEC considered the bidder's international experience that were unrelated to the bidding requirement. ⚠<br>• The BEC incorrectly computed the years of relevant work experience based on the submitted curriculum vitae.<br>• The BEC incorrectly concluded that a bidder was compliant with the experience requirements when the documents supporting the bidder's work experience showed only partial compliance. ⚠ |

Legend: ⚠ = indicative of potential misrepresentation (fraudulent practice). Fraudulent practice is any act or omission, including a misrepresentation, that knowingly or recklessly misleads, or attempts to mislead, a party to obtain a financial or other benefit or to avoid an obligation.

Source: Office of Anticorruption and Integrity, Asian Development Bank.

PROCUREMENT

CONTRACT
AND ASSET
MANAGEMENT

FINANCIAL
MANAGEMENT

OTHER
VULNERABILITIES

## Box 1: Cases—Bid Evaluation Errors

### Case 1: Civil Works Contracts Vulnerable to Unsuccessful Delivery of Project Output Due to Bid Evaluation Errors

The proactive integrity review (PIR) noted irregularities in the evaluation of bids for contract packages A and B totaling about $250 million under a large-scale project awarded to the same contractor.

***Bidder's understated contract commitments.*** The winning bidder for two packages disclosed in its bids current contract commitments aggregating to approximately $3 billion. The bid evaluation committee (BEC) failed to validate this figure against the bidder's audited financial statements, which indicated outstanding construction contracts totaling $13 billion. Thus, the total amount of contract commitments that the bidder disclosed was grossly understated by about $10 billion. The winning bidder for both contract packages should not have been assessed as financially qualified.

***Nondisclosure of pending litigation information.*** The bidding documents prescribed that a bidder's total amount of pending ligation should not exceed 50% of its net worth. Bidders disclosed its compliance with this requirement by accomplishing bid Form LIT-1: Pending Litigation. The winning bidder marked the pending litigation form "no pending litigation" and indicated "not applicable" in the portion requiring litigation details. The bidder's audited financial statements, however, stated that it was a defendant in 29 lawsuits involving claims of approximately $39 million and 47 lawsuits of approximately $34 million as of 31 December 20X1 and 20X2, respectively. The BEC did not take into consideration the nondisclosure thereof by the winning bidder.

***Need for subcontractors not declared in the bid submissions.*** The bidder did not declare any need for subcontractors in its bid until the contract negotiation stage. This prevented the BEC from directly assessing and evaluating the proposed subcontractors' capacity. The contractor may not have the financial capacity to meet the requirements of the contract and hence, subcontracted certain work components at a lower price.

***Impact of evaluation errors in output.*** The impact of inadequate due diligence on bid submissions of the winning contractor surfaced during the early stages of construction and continued as the contract progressed, causing prolonged delays. At the time of the PIR asset inspection, works for packages A and B were stalled for over a year as the contractor was unable to pay the subcontractors, among other factors.

> **TAKEAWAY | CASE 1**
>
> For road network projects, failure of one or more sections will have a significant impact on the completion and successful operation of the entire road network. It is imperative for the project teams to collaborate effectively with the procuring entity to ensure transparent, competitive, and efficient procurement exercise. More importantly, BECs should thoroughly assess bid compliance with the requirements of the bidding documents so that only qualified bidders are awarded contracts.

### Case 2: Inappropriate Acceptance of Conditional Credit Lines

The bidder's credit line statement disclosed that the issuing bank's extension of credit facility to the bidder totaling about $1.5 million for a period of 3 years was dependent upon the award of contract to the bidder and was subject to the issuing bank's approvals. Therefore, the credit line was conditional. However, the BEC considered the full amount of the credit line in the evaluation of the bidder's available financial resources.

> **TAKEAWAY | CASE 2**
>
> Bidders' financial capacity should be evaluated based on their available resources at the time of bidding, which are not conditional on future events. If the declared financial resources turn out to be unavailable at the time of project implementation, there may be contractors' cash flow problems that will result in outputs that are not delivered on time or do not meet contract specifications.

*continued on next page*

**Box 1** *continued*

### Case 3: Unvalidated Experience Documentation

The construction experience criteria required bidders to have completed a contract in the last 5 years that includes construction of one tunnel with a single hole not less than 200 meters. The winning bidder submitted supporting documents for past experience on tunnel engineering, which did not indicate whether the tunnel/s completed comprise/s a single or multiple holes. The BEC did not seek clarifications from the contractor on the ambiguity.

> **TAKEAWAY** | CASE 3
>
> Validating declared experience, particularly specific experience that is relevant to the contract being procured, ensures that contracts are awarded to bidders that can complete the project outputs on time and with the intended quality.

Source: Office of Anticorruption and Integrity, Asian Development Bank.

*Inconsistent application of bid evaluation criteria.* This may give the perception of favoritism or undue influence. One example of evaluation inconsistency identified in transport PIRs is when BECs assigned different scores for the same experts proposed by multiple bidders, even though the bidders provided the same qualification information on the experts. Another example is when bids were rejected for not submitting a required document (e.g., drawings), yet the winning bidder was found to not have submitted the same document.

*Absence of documentation to support bid evaluation decisions.* The transparency of bid evaluation is diminished when evaluation conclusions are not properly documented and/or supported. Most of the related PIR findings pertain to consulting selections where shortlisting or evaluation decisions were ambiguous or unsupported by qualification criteria or a clearly defined rating system.

*Inaccuracies in bid evaluation reports.* Inadequate and unclear information in bid evaluation reports (BER) may appear to conceal erroneous or subjective assessments favoring certain bidders. Examples of inaccurate information in BERs are summarized in Table 5.

## Table 5: Examples of Inaccuracies in Bid Evaluation Reports

| Bid Evaluation Report Item | Nature of Inaccurate Information |
| --- | --- |
| Equipment | Specifications in the bid evaluation reports (BERs) differed from the specifications in the bidding documents. |
| Financial capacity | The BERs indicated that bidders submitted audited financial statements yet the bids did not include such documents. |
| Bid submission information | Erroneous information on the number, date, and location of submissions. |

Source: Office of Anticorruption and Integrity, Asian Development Bank.

*Incorrect evaluation procedure and/or scoring.* This may also give credence to perception of favoritism or improper influence. Examples of incorrect evaluation procedure and/or scoring are summarized in Table 6.

### Table 6: Examples of Incorrect Evaluation Procedure and/or Scoring

| Bid Evaluation Aspect | Nature of Incorrect Evaluation Procedure and/or Scoring |
|---|---|
| Cash flow evaluation | The bid evaluation committee did not consider current liabilities and current contract commitments in assessing a winning bidder's financial capacity.[a] |
| Scoring for associated firms/joint ventures | Only lead firms were rated, though both the lead and associated firms should be evaluated. |
| Regional experience | The bid evaluation committee disregarded the associated firm's regional experience as required in the request for proposals. |

[a] The incorrect assessment of financial capacity may have contributed to the winning bidder's failure to mobilize resources leading to the eventual contract termination.

Source: Office of Anticorruption and Integrity, Asian Development Bank.

---

**MITIGATING MEASURES**
## Vulnerabilities in Bid Evaluation

- BEC members should undergo detailed and practical hands-on training on all aspects of bid evaluation, especially due diligence, before undertaking new bid evaluation assignments. Support from ADB regional departments, supervision consultants, and engaged procurement experts is required (a checklist on how to avoid common errors/lapses in bid evaluation is on Checklist 1)

- ADB regional departments should perform rigorous reviews of BERs, particularly when the executing agency's procurement capacity is not robust or when contracts are high-value, high-risk, or complex. Rigorous review entails seeking clarifications from the executing/implementing agencies, calling in bids on a sample basis, validating evaluation report information against bids, and assessing the reasonableness of significant evaluation committee decisions.

- The executing/implementing agency should hold pre-bid meetings for high-value, high-risk, or complex procurements, where bidding requirements are carefully discussed with bidders. The BEC must consistently apply these requirements.

- The executing/implementing agency should check accuracy and completeness of information in BERs before submitting these for ADB's no-objection. For transparency, decisions made and justifications for deviations noted should be properly documented in the BERs.

## Checklist 1: How to Avoid Common Errors and Lapses in Bid Evaluation

**ADB Sanctions List**

☐ Verify that the bidder (all parties to the joint venture/association/consortium agreement) is not on ADB's complete Sanctions List (https://sanctions.adb.org).

**Construction Turnover**

☐ Verify the turnover declared on the bidding form against the turnover reported in the audited financial statements submitted.

**Financial Capacity**

☐ Verify the financial capacity-related accounts (working capital, net worth) declared on the bidding form against the corresponding accounts in the audited financial statements submitted.

☐ Verify the credit lines declared against the supporting documents submitted.

**Current Contract Commitments**

☐ Verify the current contract commitments declared on the bidding form against the contract commitments reported in the audited financial statements submitted.

**Experience**

☐ Verify the experience declared in the bidding form against the work completion certificates (for works) and curricula vitae (for experts/consultants) submitted.

**Pending Litigation**

☐ Verify the pending litigations declared on the bidding form against the pending litigation disclosures in the audited financial statements submitted.

**Criteria Requiring Computations**

☐ Recompute the amounts on the bidding forms and verify that the formula used, including the exchange rates, are correct.

ADB = Asian Development Bank, OAI = Office of Anticorruption and Integrity.

**Note**: Where a red flag is identified, refer it to OAI for further verification.

**Source**: Office of Anticorruption and Integrity, Asian Development Bank.

## (A3) Contract Award

***Contract awarded without ADB's approval.*** Awarding contracts without ADB's approval diminishes the transparency and casts doubts on the fairness of the procurement process. One example where this issue was observed was when an executing agency hired a substitute contractor without ADB's approval to perform emergency repairs on works that were supposed to be completed by a nonperforming contractor.

**MITIGATING MEASURES**
Contract Awarded Without ADB's Approval

The executing agency should award prior-review contracts only after receiving ADB's approval of the procurement decision. Post-facto approvals for prior review contracts are inappropriate and should only be sought in exceptional circumstances.

PROCUREMENT

CONTRACT
AND ASSET
MANAGEMENT

FINANCIAL
MANAGEMENT

OTHER
VULNERABILITIES

# CONTRACT AND ASSET MANAGEMENT

## B1 Contract Administration

***Unauthorized substitutions of key experts post-contract award.*** Appropriately assessing substitute experts' qualifications and ensuring proper approval is given for such substitutions reduces the risk that experts may not have the required qualifications for the position. An unqualified substitute can lead to poor-quality outputs and cost overruns. Unauthorized substitutions (commonly known as bait-and-switch) also circumvent the bid evaluation process, where the winning bid is determined based on the assessment of the qualifications of the experts nominated in the bid, among other factors.

> **MITIGATING MEASURES**
> Unauthorized Substitution of Key Experts Post-Contract Award
>
> After contract award, the executing agency should approve any substitutions of key experts before they are deployed. The approval should be (i) based on whether the substitute expert has the qualifications required (at least equal to the expert to be replaced) for the position, and (ii) properly documented.

## B2 Output Monitoring

***Use of substandard materials and works that were substandard, defective, or off-specifications.***
Executing/implementing agencies should ensure that contractors, consultants, and suppliers are adequately supervised and that any issues are addressed in a timely manner. The PIR asset inspection of transport projects identified output defects and use of substandard materials, which could have been detected and rectified earlier had the project supervision been more robust. The inadequate supervision of executing entities resulted in delays, acceptance of works that were substandard, and cost overruns. Examples of related cases that the PIR team observed are in Table 7.

### Table 7: Examples of Use of Substandard Materials and Works That Were Substandard, Defective, or Off-Specifications

| Output Deficiency | Details |
|---|---|
| Substandard materials and defective works in a road upgrading project | **Substandard and defective works, primarily due to the use of substandard materials:** <br>• Bumpy pavement of a recently completed secondary road. <br>• Potholes and complete pavement failure in several isolated locations. <br>• Embankment failures at two locations in the areas where the seal had completely deteriorated with two minor slips in road foundation cuttings. <br>• Sagging guardrails and failed embankments in some areas. |
| Off-specification works in a highway construction project | The proactive integrity review inspection team took soil samples from various sites across the five sample civil works packages for testing soil compaction. The results showed that overall soil samples were below the standard compaction rate of K=95%. The results also established that in terms of proportionate distribution to specific packages, the highest average incidence of deviation was noted in three packages: 75%, 67%, and 33%. The average incidence of deviation in one of the four packages was relatively lower at 14%. All soil samples taken from sites relating to the fifth package, however, had acceptable compaction rates. |

*continued on next page*

**Table 7** *continued*

| Output Deficiency | Details |
|---|---|
| Substandard materials and off-specification works in a regional road development project | **Defects and off-specifications based on on-site inspection and materials testing**<br>• Thinner pavement layer than initially proposed by the design consultant was installed. This was a transition-type pavement requiring rehabilitation every 4–5 years during operation.<br>• The material testing results showed that in some road sections, the sub-base and non-frost layer were unstable for the intended purpose and climatic site conditions.<br>• Construction defects, including poor compaction of road shoulders and embankment, misplaced and defective road furniture, and poor alignment and construction methods of the side drains. |
| Substandard and off-specification works in a tollway project | • Corroded shuttering and reinforcement that are not up to acceptable standards. The alignment of the shuttering needed to be rectified.<br>• Incorrect water-to-cement ratio. Based on the slump test result, water in the water-to-cement ratio was on the higher side.<br>• Unprotected approaches by stone boulders as required. As a result, the approach of the bridge washed out from the release of excess water in the upstream dam.<br>• Defective hard shoulders. The drop from the main carriageway to the hard shoulder was more than the acceptable limits. |

Source: Office of Anticorruption and Integrity, Asian Development Bank.

**MITIGATING MEASURES**
## Use of Substandard Materials and Works That Were Substandard, Defective, or Off-Specifications

• Erring contractors, consultants, and suppliers should be held accountable to ensure that they fulfill their contractual obligations. This entails enforcing relevant penalty clauses and reporting poor performance to ADB without delay.

• For decentralized, complex, or high-risk projects, independent third-party monitoring firms should be engaged to augment the monitoring activities performed by executing and/or implementing agencies, ADB regional departments, and supervision consultants.

• Executing/implementing agencies should closely monitor the supervision consultants. This entails rigorous review of the consultants' progress reports and, as necessary, verification of progress through field visits. A guide that provides a practical framework for field visits/ asset inspections can be accessed through this link: https://www.adb.org/sites/default/ files/institutional-document/431571/asset-inspection-project-integrity.pdf.

PROCUREMENT

CONTRACT
AND ASSET
MANAGEMENT

FINANCIAL
MANAGEMENT

OTHER
VULNERABILITIES

# FINANCIAL MANAGEMENT

## C1 Expenditure Management

***Ineligible expenditures.*** Executing and implementing agencies should counter the risk of payments made for ineligible expenditures. Expenditures that are (i) not within the contract terms, (ii) inadequately or inappropriately supported, or (iii) unauthorized are considered ineligible. These indicate that claims were not thoroughly reviewed against contract provisions. They provide opportunities for fraud and expose the project to the risk of loss of funds. Examples of lapses in expenditure management are summarized in Table 8. Box 2 presents sample cases of ineligible expenditures.

### Table 8: Examples of Ineligible Expenditures

| Expenditure Category | Lapse/Gap in the Expenditure |
|---|---|
| Contractor's progress billings | • Amount paid greater than the milestone payment amount in the contract<br>• Payments made prior to (i) contract award, (ii) approval of the related contract variation, and/or (iii) work completion[a]<br>• Payments made based on interim payment certificates without supporting documents<br>• Substantial payments despite slow progress ⚠<br>• Payments for claims that were not authorized by the appropriate officer, e.g., project manager |
| Consultant's remuneration | • Individual timesheets not reviewed or not attached to the claims<br>• Claims paid for nonworking days (e.g., holidays) with no documentation of pre-approval of holiday or weekend work |
| Consultant's expenses | • Travel expenses not supported by proof of travel (tickets, receipts, boarding passes)<br>• Purchase of assets unrelated to the project |
| Salaries of and advances to project management office staff | • Salary payments inconsistent with the employment contracts<br>• No supporting documents for the authorization of the advance |

[a] The review of progress reports and asset inspection detected these payments made prior to work completion.

⚠ = indicative of potential misrepresentation or fraudulent practice. Fraudulent practice is any act or omission, including a misrepresentation, that knowingly or recklessly misleads, or attempts to mislead, a party to obtain a financial or other benefit or to avoid an obligation.

Source: Office of Anticorruption and Integrity, Asian Development Bank.

### Box 2: Cases—Ineligible Expenditures

#### Case 1: Payments Made before Work Completion

Inspection of project roads for civil works contracts showed that installation of road markings was not completed in several road sections despite the flagging of the same observation in two separate joint inspections by executing agency staff and supervision consultant. Photos of affected road sections contradicted the information in the supervision consultant's

progress report. Payments for these road markings were improperly made.

**TAKEAWAY | CASE 1**
Periodic inspections of works will enable the executing agency to verify contractors' claims and supervision consultants' reports, thereby ensuring that payments are only made for works that are actually completed.

*continued on next page*

**Box 2** *continued*

### Case 2: Interim Payment Certificates without Supporting Documents

In several civil works contracts, interim payment certificates were not supported by documents that would indicate fulfillment of contractual conditions and allow payment of the second installment of the advance. The project implementation unit processed payments based on the contractors' interim payment certificates that the construction supervision consultants certified without adequate review.

**TAKEAWAY | CASE 2**

The executing agency's oversight of the supervision consultant's issuance of adequately documented and reviewed work completion certificates will ensure that claims are appropriately supported, and payments are made only for legitimate expenditures.

### Case 3: Unauthorized Payments

Several interim payment certificates were paid without endorsement of the authorized officer. The provincial works manager, who had no authority to approve payments, authorized the payments. The payment requests should have been rejected, but they were ultimately authorized after the contractor approached the secretary of the executing agency requesting payments to be expedited. It was widely held that the contractor was experiencing some liquidity issues and was seeking payments in advance. The erring provincial works manager was removed from office and transferred to a position away from any financial management responsibilities.

**TAKEAWAY | CASE 3**

Post-facto payment authorization is inappropriate as control override is susceptible to abuse.

### Case 4: Purchase of Assets Unrelated to the Project

The executing agency included in the project consultant's terms of reference the acquisition of computers and software. The computers and software were unrelated to the consultant's tasks as the consultant was responsible for road design and supervision, while the software application was a budget and expense system for personal services maintenance and capital outlays.

**TAKEAWAY | CASE 4**

Periodic inspection of project assets is essential to ensure that they are used only for project-related activities.

### Case 5: Ineligible Expenditures relating to Project Management Staff

The project's payments of remuneration to project management office staff members were inconsistent with their employment contracts. Without employment contracts of some project management office staff for certain years nor documentation on how individual increases were computed, the accuracy of staff salaries could not be validated.

The following lapses in the process and documentation requirements for salary advances resulted in the payment of ineligible expenditures:

- Salary advances did not have any supporting documents to signify that these were authorized.

- The payment request and check only provided the name of the person authorized to withdraw the amount requested. There was no documentation identifying the recipient of the advance payment.

- Advances were not appropriately recorded in the project accounts. These were recorded as salaries, which did not reflect the nature of the actual transactions.

**TAKEAWAY | CASE 5**

As salaries constitute a significant portion of the expenditures to run project management or implementing offices or units, they are susceptible to manipulation, e.g., salaries may be paid to ghost employees, salaries may be used as a "pass-through" for illegitimate transfers. As such, process and documentation requirements for salaries should be adhered to.

FINANCIAL MANAGEMENT

Source: Office of Anticorruption and Integrity, Asian Development Bank.

PROCUREMENT

CONTRACT
AND ASSET
MANAGEMENT

**FINANCIAL
MANAGEMENT**

OTHER
VULNERABILITIES

### 🛠️ MITIGATING MEASURES
### Ineligible Expenditures

- Before endorsing claims for payment, executing/implementing agencies should ensure that (i) payment approval procedures are followed, (ii) supporting documents are checked for accuracy and completeness, and (iii) details in the claims are validated against the contracts and supporting documents. Payments should be refused or reduced in line with relevant contractual provisions for works or services that were not performed or goods that were not delivered (a checklist on how to avoid common errors/lapses in expenditure payment processing is provided in Checklist 2).

- ADB regional departments and resident missions should ensure that executing and implementing agencies, including project implementing units/offices, understand their obligations under ADB's Anticorruption Policy, especially the obligation to report any integrity violation to OAI without delay when such is initially identified or suspected.

### Checklist 2: How to Avoid Common Errors and Lapses in Expenditure Payment Processing

**All Types**

☐ Verify the claim against the milestone payment terms stipulated in the contract (including contract variations).

☐ Check whether the payment information indicated in the claim matches with the payment information in the contract.

☐ Identify any red flags on the supporting documents submitted, e.g., erasures, alterations, or other errors and ask for clarifications.

**Works (Contractors)**

☐ Verify the claim against interim payment certificates/certificates of completion. Check if there are claims on non-workdays (work on a weekend or holiday with no preapproval).

**Services (Consultants)**

☐ Verify the remuneration claim (for input-based contracts) against detailed timesheets submitted.

☐ Verify claims for reimbursable expenses against supporting documents as required in the contract (not applicable for full lump-sum contracts), including:
  ○ Travel costs—proof of travel (tickets, receipts, boarding passes);
  ○ Accommodation—proof of stay (hotel bills, invoices, receipts); and
  ○ Seminars and workshops—attendance sheets, invoices or receipts for workshop costs like venue and equipment rental and refreshments.

**Goods (Suppliers)**

☐ Verify the claim against sales invoice and delivery receipt/proof that goods have been delivered, inspected, accepted, and, as necessary, properly installed.

Note: Where a red flag is identified, refer it to OAI for further verification.
Source: Office of Anticorruption and Integrity, Asian Development Bank.

## ◈ C2 Financial Reporting

***Inadequate and unreliable accounting systems.*** To ensure that timely and accurate financial information is provided for project implementation and progress monitoring purposes, executing and/or implementing agencies should maintain adequate and reliable project accounting systems and apply accounting standards acceptable to ADB. Inadequate and unreliable systems increase (i) the risk of undetected integrity violations, noncompliance, and other irregularities; and (ii) the risk of making an unsound project management decision based on faulty financial information. Common PIR findings for this vulnerability include failure to maintain separate project accounts, discrepancies between the project and ADB financial records, and nonperformance of bank reconciliations.

**MITIGATING MEASURES**
Inadequate and Unreliable
Accounting Systems

- Project accounts should be maintained separately from other projects and activities of executing and/or implementing agencies.

- Periodic account reconciliations between (i) project accounts and ADB financial records and (ii) project accounts and bank records should be performed monthly or quarterly, as necessary and practicable, and any discrepancies should be immediately resolved.

# OTHER INTEGRITY-RELATED VULNERABILITIES THAT CUT ACROSS PROJECT IMPLEMENTATION PROCESSES

Integrity risks in project implementation principally result from capacity gaps by the executing and/or implementing agency—particularly in procurement, contract and asset management, financial management processes, and in maintaining project records.

## D1 | Capacity of Executing and Implementing Agency

*Inadequate technical capacity on ADB operational guidelines and procedures.* Project staff of executing and implementing agencies should be knowledgeable on ADB procurement, financial management, and disbursement guidelines and procedures. Given the observed frequent staff turnover and high dependence on consultants, executing and implementing agencies should ensure that this institutional knowledge is retained, transferred, and refreshed.

**MITIGATING MEASURES**
Staff Capacity Issues

To ensure that institutional knowledge and practices over ADB operational guidelines and procedures are retained, transferred, and refreshed, executing and implementing agencies, with assistance from ADB as necessary, should develop an onboarding kit for new staff that includes primers and manuals. Regular relevant trainings should be undertaken for all staff and a quality assurance or monitoring process should be implemented under the guidance or assistance from ADB as required.

## D2 | Records Management

*Missing or disorganized key project records and absence of suitable records management.* Inaccurate or incomplete audit trail of project activities complicates the timely prevention and detection of integrity violations, noncompliance, and errors. Executing and implementing agencies should maintain an effective records management system that evidences their compliance with anticorruption, procurement, financial management, and other relevant guidelines.

**MITIGATING MEASURES**
Records Management Issues

Executing and implementing agencies should establish and maintain an effective system of records management to (i) facilitate records identification, validation, storage, and retrieval; (ii) improve accountability; (iii) drive timely detection of errors and irregularities; and (iv) prevent misplacement.

# CONCLUSION

Through its proactive integrity reviews of 31 transport projects, ADB's Office of Anticorruption and Integrity identified vulnerabilities and red flags in (i) procurement, (ii) contract and asset management, and (iii) financial management processes. Key vulnerabilities are summarized in Table 9.

To manage related risks, ADB encourages project staff to apply the mitigating measures recommended in this publication and use the due diligence checklists for bid evaluation (Checklist 1) and expenditure payment processing (Checklist 2). Project staff must remain alert to red flags of integrity violations and report suspected violations to the Office of Anticorruption and Integrity.

Integrity risks are generally elevated in complex, decentralized projects (i.e., large-scale projects involving numerous project

components, geographical locations, and implementing entities). These projects benefit from strong accountability and control mechanisms that clarify responsibilities at each implementation level (from the executing agency down to the last implementing unit), and from closer supervision by the executing agency and ADB. Integrity-related controls should be embedded in contracts, manuals, and other authoritative documents.

Under Operational Priority 7 of Strategy 2030, ADB has committed to support governments in their efforts to eradicate corruption and to implement anticorruption measures in all its projects and programs. We trust that the insights compiled in this publication will contribute to these endeavors.

## Table 9: High- and Medium-Risk Vulnerabilities in Transport Projects and their Implications

| Process | Subprocess | Vulnerability | Risk Implication |
|---|---|---|---|
| **Procurement** | A1 **Bidding** | Red flags of collusion among bidders and unmanaged conflict of interest | Conflicts of interest, and fraud and corruption, jeopardizing the project and alienating prospective bidders |
| | A2 **Bid evaluation** | Inadequate due diligence, inconsistent application of bid evaluation criteria, absence of documentation to support bid evaluation decisions, inaccuracies in bid evaluation reports, and incorrect evaluation procedure and/or scoring | Diminished transparency and fairness of the bid evaluation subprocess resulting in contract awards to unqualified bidders |
| | A3 **Contract award** | Contracts awarded without ADB's approval | Diminished transparency and fairness of the contract award subprocess |
| **Contract and asset management** | B1 **Contract administration** | Unauthorized substitution of key experts post-contract award | Circumvention of the bid evaluation process that may result in the hiring of unqualified experts leading to poor quality outputs and cost overruns |
| | B2 **Output monitoring** | Use of substandard materials and acceptance of works that were substandard, defective, or off-specifications resulting from the inadequate monitoring of contractors by executing/implementing agencies and supervision consultants | Implementation delays, inferior quality of outputs, and cost overruns |
| **Financial management** | C1 **Expenditure management** | Ineligible, unsupported, or inaccurate expenditures being paid resulting from weaknesses in the review and analysis of claims | Heightened opportunities for fraud resulting in potential loss of project funds; potential threat to subsequent maintenance or warranty claims |
| | C2 **Financial reporting** | Inadequate and unreliable accounting systems | Greater risk of not detecting integrity violations, noncompliance, and other irregularities |
| | | | Flawed project management decisions based on inaccurate financial information |

ADB = Asian Development Bank
Source: Office of Anticorruption and Integrity, Asian Development Bank.

# APPENDIX List of Proactive Integrity Reviews of Transport Projects

| Country | Project | PIR Report Issuance Date |
|---|---|---|
| Afghanistan | Emergency Infrastructure Rehabilitation and Reconstruction Project | Feb 2009 |
| Armenia | Rural Road Sector Project | Dec 2009 |
| Azerbaijan | Road Network Development Program - Projects 1 and 2[a] | Dec 2014 |
| Cambodia | Greater Mekong Subregion: Cambodia Northwest Provincial Road Improvement Project | Sep 2012 |
| | Rural Roads Improvement Project and Rural Roads Improvement Project II[a] | Sep 2016<br>Aug 2017 (follow-up) |
| Fiji | Third Fiji Road Upgrading Sector Project | Aug 2006 |
| India | Jaipur Metro Rail Line 1-Phase B Project | Jan 2017<br>May 2018 (follow-up) |
| | Surat–Manor Tollway Project | Mar 2005 |
| Kazakhstan | Central Asia Regional Economic Cooperation (CAREC) Transport Corridor I (Zhambyl Oblast Section) [Western Europe–Western PRC International Transit Corridor 1] Investment Program - Project 1 | Jul 2011 |
| | CAREC Corridors 1 and 6 Connector Road (Aktobe–Makat) Reconstruction Project | Jun 2020 |
| Mongolia | Regional Road Development Project | Oct 2013 |
| Myanmar | Greater Mekong Subregion East–West Economic Corridor Eindu to Kawkareik Road Improvement Project | Jun 2017 |
| | Maubin–Phyapon Road Rehabilitation Project | Jun 2017 |
| Nepal | Air Transport Capacity Enhancement Project | May 2014 |
| | Subregional Transport Enhancement Project | Oct 2014 |
| Papua New Guinea | Community Water Transport Project | Feb 2010 |
| | Road Maintenance and Upgrading Sector Project | Jan 2006 |
| | Bridge Replacement for Improved Rural Access Sector Project | Aug 2017<br>Dec 2019 (follow-up) |
| | Highlands Region Road Improvement Investment Program - Projects 1 and 2[a] | Oct 2017<br>Feb 2019 (follow-up) |
| People's Republic of China | Dali–Lijiang Railway Project | Jan 2007 |
| | Hunan Roads Development III Project | Feb 2011 |
| Philippines | Metro Manila Air Quality Improvement Sector Project - Investment Component | Nov 2006 |
| Philippines | Road Improvement and Institutional Development Project | Dec 2015 |
| Sri Lanka | Roads Network Improvement Project | Jul 2003 |
| Tajikistan | CAREC Corridor 6 (Ayni–Uzbekistan Border Road) Improvement Project | Mar 2016 |
| Timor-Leste | Road Network Upgrading and Road Network Upgrading (Sector) Projects | Jan 2017<br>Dec 2018 (follow-up) |
| Viet Nam | Greater Mekong Subregion: Kunming–Hai Phong Transport Corridor - Noi Bai–Lao Cai Highway Project | Oct 2012<br>Oct 2016 (follow-up) |
| | Third Roads Improvement Project | Jul 2006 |

PIR = proactive integrity review.

Notes: Full PIR reports started to be published only in 2008. PIR reports prior to 2008 published on the Asian Development Bank (ADB) website only contain report abstracts/summaries.

ADB placed on hold its assistance in Myanmar effective 1 February 2021 and in Afghanistan effective 15 August 2021. ADB Statement on Afghanistan | Asian Development Bank (published on 10 November 2021). Manila.

[a] PIR covered two projects.

Source: Office of Anticorruption and Integrity, Asian Development Bank.